Inspiring Women of the Bible

A devotional for successful daily living

Judith R. Purkiss

O&U
Onwards & Upwards

Onwards and Upwards Publishers

4 The Old Smithy, London Road, Rockbeare, EX5 2EA, UK.

www.onwardsandupwards.org

First edition, published in the United Kingdom by Onwards and Upwards Publishers (2023).

ISBN: 978-1-78815-891-6
Editor: Sheri Newton
Typeface: Sabon LT

The views and opinions expressed in this book are the author's own, and do not necessarily represent the views and opinions of Onwards and Upwards Publishers or its staff.

ABOUT THE AUTHOR

Judith Purkiss lives in London, where she works in a secondary school as the Special Educational Needs Coordinator (SENCO), a teacher working with children who have complex additional learning needs.

Judith studied languages and has always loved the power of words – spoken or written – to inspire, motivate and transform. As a writer, Judith has been on a journey. Her first book, *Words of Encouragement*, was a labour of love – about two years in the making. The book started out as a blog and grew into a collection of daily devotional readings. It is all about encouraging those who encourage and support others; there are people who help others but have nowhere to turn themselves when they are in need.

Inspiring Women of the Bible grew from *Words of Encouragement*. This new book seeks to recognise the unsung heroines, the familiar and not so familiar women who are featured in the Bible. These are older women, poor women, outcasts, foreign women, women with dubious reputations; yet they all had in common that their eyes were on the Lord. Judith hopes that you will be able to find yourself in these pen portraits, and that you will draw strength from their courage in the face of adversity. Be encouraged, be blessed – but above all, be inspired in your walk with God.

If you wish to contact Judith, you can do so as follows:

Post: Judith R. Purkiss, c/o Onwards and Upwards Publishers Ltd., 4 The Old Smithy, London Road, Rockbeare, EX5 2EA.

Email: *judith_purkiss@hotmail.com*

Facebook: Search for 'Judith Purkiss'

ENDORSEMENT

Inspiring Women of the Bible is a treasure chest of seemingly ordinary women – for the most part. Their specialness comes to light as these women of varied backgrounds and sometimes questionable moral or social pedigree have their faith tested to a near breaking point.

Their story highlights divine attributes like wisdom, strength, mercy, impartiality, sovereignty and timely interventions. It also underscores the growth that attends anyone in a redemptive association with the Divine: understanding one's worth in the sight of God, faith, hope, boldness, obedience and altruism.

This book by Judith Purkiss is as inspiring as the inspired women of God that it describes!

Jacqueline B. Laguerre MD, RN

CONTENTS

FOREWORD BY OTIS LEWIS

It is a privilege for me to have known Sister Judith Purkiss for the past two years as a parishioner. The author is a teacher by profession and head of department at her school, which gives her a unique perspective. As a pastor of a church in Peckham, I have not only seen Sister Judith flourish in her role as family life leader (which includes women ministries leader), but also as one of the music leaders in the church. She is also developing in her role as a preacher. She has a very good knowledge of the word of God and spiritual matters. Therefore, Sister Judith is well-placed to write this book on women in the Bible. Judith has done her research and, as such, she is a good candidate for this worthwhile exploration of the lives of some female spiritual role models.

God has done so much for the world through women and has evidenced this in the Bible. For example, women have been queens, judges, prophets, evangelists and businesswomen. A woman, Mary Magdalene, was the first evangelist declaring the good news of a risen Saviour. Additionally, one should note that a woman, Mary the mother of Jesus, prompted the first miracle of Jesus, and the Lord was comfortable telling a woman that He is the Messiah.

It is very refreshing to read about women of the Bible from the perspective of a godly woman within a contemporary setting. The author's work is really clear and concise. Evidently, this is a must read; it will challenge the reader and uncover new views through the writer's lenses. Therefore, I am personally recommending this powerful book to you, the reader.

Otis Lewis
Pastor

INTRODUCTION

Why 'Inspiring Women of the Bible'?

This book is designed to help women of all ages and backgrounds get started on a journey of fruitful daily living. The devotional seeks to help you see how in circumstances that seemed impossible, faithful women of the Bible overcame many challenges in the Lord's strength. They met with the challenges of feeling alone and overwhelmed, being doubted and gossiped about. They faced the struggles of debt, infertility and being widowed. They were women just like you and me, and God intervened in their lives.

There are many different situations that you might identify with throughout these studies.

- Have you ever been the 'other woman'? If your child's father has abandoned you and your former partner's wife is sending threats, then Hagar's story is for you.
- Have you felt inferior to others for having fertility issues? If you've longed for a child, had investigation after investigation and still been unable to conceive, Manoah's wife, Hannah and Elizabeth understand how you feel.
- Have you ever lived on the margins of society because of your choices and the situations that life has thrust upon you? Rahab and the woman at the well in Samaria knew all about being used and abused by men; perhaps you can learn from their experiences.
- Do the challenges behind you seem nothing in comparison to what lies ahead? If you know you must act and if other people are depending on you, then take a leaf from Esther's book. You are where you are for such a time as this.
- Are you living in a foreign country, a widow or a lone parent? If you are struggling to pay the bills and just barely surviving, learn from Ruth and the widow with the oil. God has more than you ever imagined and He will meet your needs.

It may be that you are not regularly reading the Bible at the moment. If so, this journal can help you begin that journey. It's my hope that what you start here will inspire you to continue building your relationship with

God through reading and accepting His Word, and enjoying living the way He intended, throughout the rest of your life.

Each day you will be introduced to a woman of the Bible, and will be offered questions for reflection and space to write down your thoughts. Each individual story is a lesson for today's woman. I invite you to laugh, cry, understand and share in the experiences of these women of tremendous courage and faith. You will be inspired.

Let's get started!

1

HAGAR

THE OTHER WOMAN

Then God opened her eyes, and she saw a well of water.
Genesis 21:19 (NKJV)

Hagar had been thrown out by Abraham along with their son Ishmael. All Hagar had to survive on was a bottle of water and some food in a backpack, which guilt had caused Abraham to give to her. Hagar and Ishmael wandered into the desert of Beersheba. When their water ran out, Hagar put Ishmael under one of the bushes. Then she went off and sat down nearby, for she thought, "I cannot watch the boy die." [Gen.21:16] As she sat there, she began to cry. First disrespected, then abandoned and now in a wilderness with no water… It must have been hard to stop the tears from flowing.

Are you living with daily reminders of the bad choices you've made and finding that you must live with the bitter consequences? Have you come to the absolute end? You thought you were part of a promise, but somehow you have wound up kicked out of your home, forced to start all over again, and the little you were given to sustain you has been used up?

The angel of the Lord called to Hagar from heaven and said to her, "What is the matter, Hagar? Do not be afraid; God has heard the boy's voice. Pick him up and take him by the hand, for I will make him into a great nation." [Gen.21:17-18] Hagar's tears could have been of regret, bitterness or rage at her situation. God still wanted to know what was really wrong. God still hears prayers and He keeps His promises. His Word cannot be invalidated by deserts or thirst. Nor is it thwarted by other people's vindictive actions. God has plans to make greatness come out of what you put down to die. God opened Hagar's eyes and she saw a well of water. She went and filled the bottle with water and gave the boy a drink.

Have you given up hope and been crying so hard over what you fear will happen next that you don't see the well God has provided for you? It is near to the proposed burial site. God's word for the abandoned woman was, "What's the matter? Don't be afraid, I have heard the crying and the prayers. Pick up the promise and grasp it. Let Me open your eyes so that you can see the well I have provided for you."

Over To You...

Have you ever been abandoned by a partner or someone you love? Or have you made some poor choices, which you now regret?

_____

_____

What can you learn from Hagar's experience with God?

_____

_____

_____

_____

_____

Have you taken the time to talk to God about how you are feeling? Write down some of the things you would like to tell Him.

_____

_____

_____

_____

_____

2

MARY AND MARTHA

THE BUSY HOMEMAKER'S STORY

Jesus answered and said to her, "Martha, Martha, you are worried and troubled about many things."

Luke 10:41 (NKJV)

Martha was preparing a meal for a special Guest and only the finest cuisine would do. The honoured Guest had not made any special requests; the pressure to perform and to produce spectacular results came from within. Initially Mary, Martha's sister, drifted in and out of the kitchen, annoyingly lifting saucepan lids and sticking a spoon in "just to taste"; then the Guest arrived and Mary disappeared. As a good hostess, Martha wanted to time the different dishes to be ready simultaneously and she really needed a hand in the kitchen. With clenched teeth, she peeped into the living room and saw Mary just sitting there at Jesus' feet like one of the guests. Mary's eyes were transfixed on Jesus. A few minutes later, Martha went back to look at the group of people reclining in the living room and a sense of injustice hit her. Here she was, cooking and cleaning and planning for everyone else, but who was helping her? As Mary showed no sign of moving, Martha decided to make her own move. She went to Jesus and said, "Lord, don't You care that my sister has left me to do the work by myself? Tell her to help me." [Lk.10:40]

Are you the person that everyone turns to when they are planning a function? The one who is up to the elbows in work but cannot expect any help from anyone? Be honest: has the role of cook, housekeeper, budget planner, organiser, carer, events manager and everything else begun to grate on you? You may feel tired of being almost invisible to the guests and people who flock to you just to use your time, facilities and resources. Others don't seem to care how you feel. They don't seem to notice that you need a break. Those who are meant to help you sit down and watch you work. You cry out to God at how unfair life is and tell Him that you have too much to do and no one to help you.

Take your complaint to Jesus. "Jesus answered, 'Martha, Martha, you are worried and upset about many things, but only one thing is needed.'" [Lk.10:41-42]

Over To You...

Does the daily routine of life stress you out? In what ways?

_____

_____

_____

_____

_____

How does this affect your attitude to family and friends?

_____

_____

_____

Is it possible that you have forgotten about the most important things in life? If so, how can you focus more on those things?

_____

_____

_____

_____

3

MARY AND MARTHA (II)

THE WILLING DISCIPLE

But one thing is needed, and Mary has chosen that good part, which will not be taken away from her.

Luke 10:42 (NKJV)

I listen carefully to what God the LORD is saying, for he speaks peace to his faithful people.

Psalm 85:8 (NLT)

Wait... Jesus seemed to be commending Mary for her work avoidance! And what exactly is the one thing that is needed? It seems shocking that Mary, with her lack of effort around the house, manages to get that one thing. Significantly, how did Martha with all her hard work manage to miss out on it? Perhaps it comes down to priorities. Have you ever been so caught up in what Jesus says in His Word that everyday things like meals, management responsibilities and guests just didn't matter? The world will not come to a screeching halt if you are not there supervising everything as well as being hands-on with your work. It won't really matter if there are not three courses to eat at your table. Everything won't fall apart if you are unable to execute every detail of your perfectly laid plans.

If you are troubled, worried or upset about many things, it's worth reflecting on whether you are seeking after the better part. Le Cordon Bleu cooking is excellent and speaks volumes about the chef. But what about the real food? Not ground provisions instead of delicate pastries, but the food Jesus talked about when He said, "My food is to do the will of Him who sent Me..." [Jn.4:34 (NKJV)]. The manual or recipe book for your life may have dust on it at present, but it needs to be read regularly. Daily. Don't you want to just feast on His Word? Listen to what He says. God promises peace, hope and joy in a world which is

17

filled with conflict and is so desperately lacking in hope. Don't you just want some peace? Let go of the demands and expectations you place on yourself, as much as those imposed by others. Some things can wait. Some things ought not to be done at all. Who needs starched tablecloths, when the Master is in the house? Will anyone even notice that all the crockery is matching or that all your performance targets are met? Don't be worried and upset about many things... Go to the place where Jesus is speaking and listen to His words. Look at the ones seated at His feet, who have chosen the better part... Then join them.

Over To You

What drives you to be a perfectionist?

_____

_____

_____

_____

_____

Do you make time to feast on the Word of God?

_____

_____

Do you allow your responsibilities to get in the way of your relationship with Christ?

_____

_____

_____

_____

4

RAHAB

A SHINING LIGHT IN THE RED-LIGHT DISTRICT!

By faith the harlot Rahab did not perish with those who did not believe, when she had received the spies with peace.

Hebrews 11:31 (NKJV)

...for the LORD your God, He is God in heaven above and on earth beneath.

Joshua 2:11 (NKJV)

Rahab had opened the door to two men who required lodging for the night. These two visitors to the local brothel were different; they had not come for a night out in the town away from their wives. They were on a fact-finding mission. Rahab let the men know that she had heard about their mission. However, more importantly, Rahab wanted to tell the men that she had heard about the miraculous parting of the Red Sea and knew about the mighty power of God. Rahab did not need to experience or see miracles first-hand; hearing was enough. Rahab believed.

It is amazing to consider that although the miraculous may have become mundane in our eyes, God's actions still leave those considered 'unbelievers' in awe! While the Israelites were complaining about the catering arrangements in the desert, the people of Jericho were trembling as God created paths in the sea. When was the last time you wondered at the majesty of God? We need to have spiritual discernment and insight to recognise God moving, even when we do not fully understand all He is doing. Let us ask Him to open our eyes so we can see how He has intervened, overhauled and manifested His grace in the lives of others. Let us ask for hearts and minds that remember all He does for us daily.

It can be so easy to keep to ourselves all that we have seen, heard and experienced of God. How many people know that God is God in heaven and on earth because you say so? Who else knows and is aware of your testimony? Ironically, it took the example of a non-Israelite to reveal the work of God to the two spies. Rahab was an unlikely witness but one who believed God and His Word, and she took care to let them know this. She certainly wasn't the sort of person you could comfortably introduce to your family; indeed sometimes the Lord's messenger might not be the person we expect. We should be open to hearing of God through others, and also open to sharing with others what He has done for us. Just like the Israelites in the book of Joshua, we can say that God has led us, God has protected us and God has given us a new territory.

Over To You

When was the last time you wondered at the majesty of God?

_____

_____

What stops us sharing all that God has done for us with others?

_____

_____

_____

_____

_____

With whom can you share your story of how God delivered you?

_____

_____

_____

_____

_____

_____

5

THE WIDOW

FACE YOUR BAILIFFS – EXPERIENCE GOD'S SUFFICIENCY

"Your maidservant has nothing in the house but a jar of oil."
2 Kings 4:2 (NKJV)

Bailiffs are not known for their sensitivity or sense of timing, so the visit to this woman's house right after her husband's funeral was not entirely unexpected in 2 Kings 4. The bailiffs had come to collect on the outstanding debts of her late husband. The woman turned to Elisha the prophet in desperation. Maybe you been left having to pay back someone else's debt. It is hard enough trying to deal with your own issues; it is so difficult to deal with the fallout of the shortcomings of others. Elisha spoke to the distraught woman. "How can I help you? Tell me, what do you have in your house?" The woman replied that she did not have anything at all in the house except a little oil. Elisha instructed the woman to borrow empty jars from her neighbours and to make sure that she did not ask for just a few. Then he said that she should go inside, shut the door behind her and keep pouring oil into all the jars until each one was full. Then she should put them aside. The woman did as the prophet said. When all the borrowed jars were full, she said to her son, "Bring me another one." He replied, "There aren't any jars left." Then the oil stopped flowing.

Are you in a spiritual, financial, physical or emotional recession? It feels like every creditor is lining up to take back what is theirs, as well as what isn't. Have you cried out for help? God's response is twofold: "How can I help you?" and "What do you have in your house?" You may think that what you have is nothing much or not enough, but it is what you have. *Sometimes you need to be reduced to nothing, so that God can bless you.* Work with God on what you have to hand. How big is your faith? Do you have a growth mindset? Maximise your borrowing of containers.

Things may look grim to outsiders; the bank, the credit card and utility companies may all be clamouring for a piece of your leftovers. Loan sharks of an emotional and financial nature may be circling, but simply get on with the instructions, close your door on them and keep pouring. You have the greatness of God's Spirit within you and your vessels cannot contain it. Experience the outpouring of God's abundance into your insufficiency. What you have will be enough to satisfy all of those making demands on you and you will have resources left over. Prove God now. When He pours out blessings, there will not be containers enough to receive them.

Over To You

In what ways can you identity with the widow?

_____

_____

_____

_____

How does her story strengthen your faith?

_____

_____

_____

_____

Do you trust God to supply whatever you need?

_____

_____

_____

_____

6

ESTHER

FOR SUCH A TIME AS THIS

"If you remain completely silent at this time, relief and deliverance will arise for the Jews from another place, but you and your father's house will perish. Yet who knows whether you have come to the kingdom for such a time as this?"

Esther 4:14 (NKJV)

Esther was a Jewish exile in Persia; she had won a beauty contest and had become queen. Now the Jews were facing annihilation by Haman, a courtier who hated God's people. With this knowledge, Esther had a difficult decision to make. She could choose to identify with the people of God and risk annihilation, or remain silent and watch the destruction of her people. Mordecai, Esther's older cousin, who had brought her up as his own daughter, asked Esther to intervene. Esther offered a reasonable explanation as to why she could not simply turn up at the court and ask the king to halt the planned massacre of the Jews. You just don't walk into the presence of the king and tell him to change government policy! Mordecai let Esther know that she would not be exempt from Haman's murderous plans.

Consider the situations that God has positioned you in. Are you in an elevated position of leadership and authority? Think of all the people who were your neighbours, your peers at school, your colleagues and associates and your family members. How are they? Are they facing annihilation by poverty, illness, crime, isolation or social exclusion? It may be tempting to hide yourself from their plight and forget that you were once in their situation. It certainly feels easier to look away, concealing yourself and your Christian identity because your situation is much better now. But just like in Esther's case, because your life is better now, it doesn't mean you will escape the onslaught of attacks on God's people. If you do keep quiet, *God always has His alternatives.* Deliverance and empowerment of God's people will come; but who knows whether God has placed you where you are today to help in this specific situation? Do you see that there is something that needs to be done about the dire situation of God's people? What has God called you to do? Deliverance could come from somewhere else, but it need not. Don't wait for another opportunity to be an instrument in God's Hands. You have been chosen by Him and blessed with time, resources and talents. Use them wisely. Of course, it is a scary prospect to challenge the status quo, but God will be with you as you work for Him. Step out in faith. Who knows whether you have been placed here for such a time as this?

Over To You

In what areas of life do you have a position of leadership or responsibility?

_____

_____

_____

_____

_____

What needs of God's people do you see around you? Are you willing to challenge the status quo?

_____

_____

_____

_____

_____

Spend some time praying that God would use you "for such a time as this".

7

DEBORAH

WHAT ARE YOU WAITING FOR?

*Barak said to her, "If you will go with me, then I will go; but
if you will not go with me, I will not go!"*

Judges 4:8 (NKJV)

Israel was living under Canaanite oppression. The judge of Israel at
that time was a woman called Deborah. Deborah sent for Barak, a
young man from the tribe of Naphtali. She said to him, "Hasn't God
commanded you to go up to Mount Tabor and to take ten thousand men
from the tribes of Naphtali and Zebulun with you? God says, 'Do this
and I will have Sisera, the captain of Jabin's army, muster his army there
with all of his chariots and I will deliver them into your hand.'" Barak
replied, "If you will go with me then I will go; but if you are not going,
then I am not going either." Deborah replied, "I will go with you, but
you will not get the glory out of this. The Lord will deliver Sisera into the
hands of a woman." Barak went and rallied his men and Deborah went
with him.

You too may have been feeling the brunt of years of oppression in
your life. When you look at what seems to overwhelm you, you see that
the opposition seems to have all the advantages. *God may want you to
be the source of His deliverance to others.*

When Sisera, the commander of the Canaanite army, learnt that
Barak had gone up to Mount Tabor, he mustered his iron chariots and
went to the River Kishon.

Deborah saw the approaching army and said to Barak, "Get up; this
is the day that the Lord has delivered Sisera into your hand. God has
gone out ahead of you." [Jdg.4:14] God gave Barak victory over the
Canaanite army to the extent that Sisera left his chariot and escaped on
foot. Sisera ran to the tent of Heber, his neighbour, and sought refuge

with Heber's wife, Jael. He hid under a sheet and went to sleep. But Jael drove a tent peg into his temple as he slept. When Barak and his army turned up looking for Sisera, Jael was able to say, "Come and see the man you are looking for!"

No matter what the obstacle is in your life, or how overwhelming the odds may be, God has equipped you. You need to seek God's empowering and His perspective on your troubles. Having a mountain view will change your perspective on your problems. If you lack the courage to face your battles alone, go with someone who hears from God. Do not worry that you are poorly equipped for your mission. Sisera had chariots; Jael only had a tent peg. God will use the Jaels and the Deborahs in your life as enabling forces. Listen to them and deploy their skills and vision. You may well be a Deborah yourself, seeing potential in others. Just know that whenever God has called you to do something for Him, He has gone out ahead of you and will deliver you.

Over To You

In what situations do you feel like you are facing overwhelming odds?

Are you worried that you are not fully equipped for your role? How does Judges 4 help with your fears?

Spend some time praying for the right people to come and help you, and also for insight to see the potential in others.

8

GOMER

YOU'RE WORTH IT!

"Go, love a woman who has a lover and is an adulteress, just as the LORD loves the people of Israel, though they turn to other gods and love raisin cakes."

Hosea 3:1 (NRSV)

What are you worth? Don't go and look at your life insurance policy or calculate the value of all of your assets; just name a price. Hosea had some spending to do. God told Hosea to marry a woman who had not only a complex relationship history, but also some unresolved matters in the present. Gomer could not sustain the relationship. Even though she had married Hosea, the attraction of her former lifestyle lured her back into prostitution. Now here was God telling Hosea to love Gomer just as much as God Himself loved her.

Gomer had met the wrong man. He had used and abused her, and then he put her up for sale. Hosea had to go and buy Gomer back. "So I bought her for fifteen pieces of silver and a measure and a half of barley." [Hos.3:2] The price of a slave was thirty pieces of silver [Ex.21:32], so in effect Hosea bought Gomer at a reduced price. Her association with her former lifestyle had devalued her. However, it was all that Hosea could afford. He had to make up the price with some sacks of grain, giving everything that he had. God gave everything for us: the life of His Son. Your worth is much more than that of a slave: "For you know that it was not with perishable things such as silver or gold that you were redeemed from the empty way of life handed down to you from your ancestors, but with the precious blood of Christ." [1Pet.1:18-19 (NIV)]

So what is your worth? God alone could pay the ultimate price for you. Are you worth it? Well, in human terms, we are all second-hand goods. You may have been trapped by your past, or still be trapped in your present. But God's word for you is that even if no one else wants you, even if everyone else has used you up and discarded you, He says, "I love you." He says, "You are worth the ultimate price!" God was willing to send His Son to die for us. His love is not a temporary feeling; rather, God says that His love is limitless and eternal.

Perhaps you are tired of life on the shelf. Perhaps you are desperately waiting for the right person to come along. He's here. God has been trawling the aisles of your life, looking for you. It doesn't matter how much life has devalued you and marked you down as worthless, God is there willing to pay whatever it takes. When He pays the price, He will keep you with Him in a bond of everlasting love and kindness; battered, bruised and discarded – yet costing God His most precious Son. You're worth it.

Over To You

If you have been used and abused by the men in your life, how has that left you feeling about yourself?

_____

_____

_____

_____

Do you need God to help you choose the right relationships? (If you do, ask Him for wisdom!)

_____

_____

_____

_____

How does Gomer's experience show you how much God loves you?

_____

_____

_____

_____

_____

9

NAOMI

SURVIVING A BITTER EXPERIENCE

"Don't call me Naomi," she told them. "Call me Mara because the Almighty has made my life very bitter. I went away full, but the LORD has brought me back empty."

Ruth 1:20-21 (NIV)

There was a famine in Israel. Naomi and her husband Elimelech migrated to Moab in search of a better life. Their two sons had travelled with them. The sons both married local girls. In time Elimelech and his two sons died. Naomi found herself a widow with two widowed daughters-in-law. She heard that the famine was over in Israel because God had visited His people and given them food. When she heard that life was now better there, Naomi decided to return home.

Have you ever looked at your situation and thought that absolutely everyone has life easier than you do? They have good jobs, savings, drive bigger cars, live in better houses, enjoy good health, their children are just a pleasure and they seem to be living the perfect existence. Then you look at yourself. Maybe you have a dead-end job, maybe you're living in overdraft, with a car that routinely breaks down and a house that needs major repairs. Perhaps diabetes, hypertension and cancer have ravaged your family. Perhaps your children's school calls every day informing you of what's gone wrong today. Perhaps you just feel your existence is hellish.

Is it time to move and start all over again? You may be tempted to chase after material prosperity. Changing our circumstances, maybe even our address, may work for a while, but eventually you will find that what you were seeking was back at home all along. Disobedience to the will of God inevitably leads to famine, but in due time, God will visit His people and meet their needs.

As Naomi returned to Bethlehem, the whole town speculated about whether it was really her. She replied, "Don't call me Naomi ... the Almighty has made my life very bitter. I went away full, but the LORD has brought me back empty." [Rt.1:20-21 (NIV)] Are you angry with God? Like Naomi, you may feel bitterness and resentment towards Him because of how your life has turned out. Oh friend, don't wait until you have experienced death, destruction and loss before you realise that God has given you fullness of life with Him. Don't wait till you lose everything else to find true value and meaning in life. There is hope, there is planned fulfilment of God's promises – no matter where you are, you will hear that God has visited His people and provided for them. Go back home to God. It may be bitter for you, people will gossip and raise questions, but just wait and see what God will do for you at the time of the harvest.

Over To You

Have you allowed hard times to make you bitter and resentful?

_____

_____

_____

_____

In what ways does God constantly provide for His people?

_____

_____

_____

_____

_____

_____

Do you need to make a journey to your spiritual home?

_____

_____

_____

_____

10

RUTH

JUST LIKE STARTING OVER

"May the LORD repay you for what you have done. May you be richly rewarded by the LORD, the God of Israel, under whose wings you have come to take refuge."

Ruth 2:12 (NIV)

Starting a new job is a challenge; moving house is equally so. Moving to a new country, where the language, customs and religion are completely different from your own, is daunting. Doing all three simultaneously is inviting stress – but this is what Ruth did. Ruth began working in a field gleaning after the harvesters to support herself and her mother-in-law, Naomi. It happened that she began to work in the field of one of Naomi's relatives, a man named Boaz. When Boaz came by to check the progress of the harvest, he noticed Ruth toiling away in the fields. He enquired about who she was and, having heard her name, realised that this was the girl who featured in the Bethlehem rumour mill. She was that foreign girl who had travelled back from Moab with Naomi. Boaz called Ruth to himself and spoke to her, telling her that she had the freedom of the field and that she should drink out of the harvesters' vessels whenever she became thirsty. Ruth thanked Boaz for his kindness to her, a foreigner. Boaz responded, "I've been told all about what you have done for your mother-in-law since the death of your husband – how you left your father and mother and your homeland and came to live with a people you did not know before. May the LORD repay you for what you have done. May you be richly rewarded by the LORD, God of Israel, under whose wings you have come to take refuge." [Rt.2:11-12 (NIV)]

Have you been widowed, divorced or had some other life-changing experience and had to move home? Often starting all over again means a new job, strange people and customs, and a new neighbourhood or country. Just as He did with Ruth, God is watching you with a loving eye. He will use the local gossips to spread abroad how hard you work. Even if you look different, dress differently from the rest and don't speak their language, let the distinction between you and your co-workers be that your work is consistently excellent. Naomi had returned to Bethlehem on hearing the news that God had visited His people. Ruth was reaping the benefits of His visit. When God visits you, are you poised ready to work to receive the things that the Lord has left for you to harvest?

Over To You

What life-changing experiences have caused you to move home?

_____

_____

_____

_____

What new challenges are you facing, perhaps at work or in another area
of life?

_____

_____

_____

_____

Are you positioning yourself for God to bless you by trusting Him and
working hard?

_____

_____

_____

_____

11

THE WIDOW OF ZAREPHATH

MOUTH-TO-HEART RESUSCITATION

Good will come to those who are generous ... Surely the righteous will never be shaken ... They will have no fear of bad news ... trusting in the LORD.

Psalm 112:5-7 (NIV)

Some time later the widow's son got sick; he got worse and worse, and finally he died.

1 Kings 17:17 (GNT)

What happens when your theology does not quite match up with your experience of living? The widow been kind to the man of God and fed him. And now this was how God repaid her kindness – by taking away her only son... The woman lost no time in coming to Elijah to demand answers. "What have I done to deserve this? Have you come to my house to remind me of my sin and kill my son?" Elijah had no answers. [1Kgs.17:17-18] The widow had obeyed God by taking in the prophet, and God had fed the entire household for a long while. Now it seemed as if Elijah would have to defend God and interpret His will. Elijah was wise not to enter into a debate with the woman about the loss of her son. He did not know why the child had died, so he did not offer any explanation. What he did do was to take the lifeless boy to God and pray.

When you have a seemingly hopeless situation in your life, when your heart is gripped by fear, anger, bitterness, shame or grief, take it to God. Don't speculate about the whys and wherefores with others; they don't know either.

Elijah performed the first recorded act of mouth-to-mouth resuscitation; God heard the anguished questions of the prophet and the urgent prayer to restore the boy's life, and the boy began breathing. Elijah

41

returned to the woman and said, "See, your child's alive!" The woman said to Elijah, "Now by this I know that you are a man of God and that *the word of the LORD in your mouth is truth.*" [1Kgs.17:24 (NKJV), emphasis added]

Suffering comes to teach us something; each lesson will be different. God had given the widow evidence of His Word, but it was not enough. The continued supply of food and water in a time of famine was evidence that His Word was true. However, this truth had not permeated the widow's soul. The death and coming back to life of her only son taught the widow that God's grace saves and His promises are sure. Do you have some tough questions for God? Are you unsure as to whether His Word is true? Let God perform some mouth-to-heart resuscitation; let His words breathe life into your soul and *then you will know that His Word is true.*

Over To You

How have experiences of loss or bereavement impacted your life and faith?

_____

_____

_____

_____

What tough questions do you have for God?

_____

_____

_____

How can you allow difficult experiences to teach you God's will for your life?

_____

_____

_____

_____

_____

12

ANNA

THE REAL DEAL

For you will forget the shame of your youth, and will not remember the reproach of your widowhood anymore. For your Maker is your husband, the LORD of hosts is His name.

Isaiah 54:4-5 (NKJV)

When a person experiences the loss of someone they loved, it is common to feel abandoned and desolate as they grieve. Where do you go for comfort? Sometimes when you look around for support, the question is not *where* do you go, but rather *to whom* can you go? God says, "Leave your fatherless children, I will preserve them alive; and let your widows trust in Me." [Jer.49:11 (NKJV)] The apostle Paul admonishes Timothy to honour those widows that are "widows indeed", or real widows, adding that a real widow is one "who is desolate, trusts in God and is continuously in prayer and supplication night and day" [1Tim.5:5]. As human beings, there is a tendency for us to categorise people in terms of those who we decide are in genuine need and those who we think are taking advantage of our compassionate nature. God makes no such distinction: "Do you have a fatherless child or children? Bring them to Me. Has your heart been broken by bereavement or loss? Trust in Me."

When Mary and Joseph brought Jesus to the temple to be blessed, they encountered a widow named Anna who worshipped there daily, devoting her time, day and night, to prayer. [Lk.2:36-37] Anna spoke a blessing into the life of the baby Jesus. Widowed from an early age, Anna could have legitimately stayed home to mourn, as she had never remarried. However, had she done this, she would have foregone the opportunity to have an encounter with the Lord Himself. When you find yourself on your own with no tangible support, when you find yourself desolate and inconsolable, when you find yourself with nowhere to go, God is inviting you to His house. God says that He is a "Father to the fatherless, who gives justice to widows in His holy habitation" [Ps.68:5].

Do you want a husband? Are you too embarrassed to tell everyone that you have needs too – that you still want love and affection? Seek God in His house. Do you want to find acceptance, support and love? Go to the place where God lives, His habitation, and pray continually. You will encounter Him there and hear words of encouragement for your life.

Over To You

Are you longing for a close and loving relationship?

_____

_____

What are some of the ways that you can seek, and find, refuge and comfort?

_____

_____

_____

_____

_____

What is God saying to you today about His Fatherly and Husbandly care for you?

_____

_____

_____

_____

_____

13

RIZPAH

VIGILANT IN HOPE

Now Rizpah the daughter of Aiah took sackcloth and spread it for herself on the rock, from the beginning of harvest until the late rains poured on them from heaven. And she did not allow the birds of the air to rest on them by day nor the beasts of the field by night.

2 Samuel 21:10 (NKJV)

During King David's reign, a devastating famine which lasted three years hit the land of Israel. David asked God for a reason. God responded that this was a judgement against the kingdom because of Saul's mistreatment of the Gibeonites. We read in 2 Samuel 21 that David asked the Gibeonites what he could do to atone for Saul's sins. They responded that they wanted to execute seven descendants of Saul. David took two of Saul's sons by Saul's concubine Rizpah and the five sons of Saul's daughter Merab and handed them over to the Gibeonites. The young men were executed at the beginning of the barley harvest and their bodies were left exposed to the elements. Rizpah took sackcloth, spread it on a rock and, until the rainy season started, she kept a vigil day and night so that birds and scavengers could not come near the bodies.

When David heard what Rizpah had done, he took the bones of Saul and Jonathan, as well as the bodies of the young men, carried them to the tomb of Kish, Saul's father, and gave them a decent burial.

Perhaps you too have you experienced loss at its most unfair and basic level. Sometimes there feels very little we can do. Rizpah could not fight for her sons because they were already dead. However, she could and did keep a vigil of loyalty for both her sons and also those of Merab. We don't know where Merab was during the vigil. We don't know why she wasn't there with her sackcloth defending those who could not defend themselves. But Rizpah's silent protest against injustice was eloquent as she protected those who have no voice. Come rain, shine, bird or wild animal, Rizpah was on guard protecting those she loved. Eventually her faithfulness propelled David into action.

Sometimes we guard our dreams long after powerful people have crushed them. We watch the lifeless embodiments of our hopes being exposed to the elements, determined that come what may, no one will ravage what we nurtured. You may not have the voice to challenge what has taken place, but by your tireless devotion, you will draw attention to what is right. It may not happen immediately, but one day the King will notice and take action.

Over To You

In what ways have you experienced loss at its most unfair and basic level?

_____

_____

_____

_____

What dreams and hopes of justice are you keeping alive?

_____

_____

_____

_____

What can you do to protect vulnerable and disadvantaged people?

_____

_____

_____

_____

_____

14

THE WIDOW PERSISTENT IN PRAYER

DON'T TAKE NO FOR AN ANSWER

"'Though I neither fear God nor respect man, yet because this widow keeps bothering me, I will give her justice, so that she will not beat me down by her continual coming.'"

Luke 18:4-5 (ESV)

In Luke 18, Jesus told a parable about a judge in a certain city who had no regard for God or for people. Also in the city was a widow who used to come before the judge and ask him to rule in her favour against someone who had wronged her. For a long while, the judge kept on ignoring the woman and her request, but she just kept on coming back, seeking justice. Eventually the judge said that he would respond to the woman because she was wearing him out with continual pleas.

There are probably things you have been praying about persistently for a long time, problems you been begging God to give you solutions to. How long should you pray before you give up? The woman in the parable had a problem and she wanted results. She may well have known that the judge could not care less about her situation, but that didn't dissuade her. She had decided that this was the man who had the power to administer justice on her behalf. Therefore, it didn't matter that he did not wish to be disturbed and could not be bothered; she had her issues and he was going to deal with them. Eventually, rather than responding out of a desire for justice, the judge responded to get rid of the noise from the woman.

Jesus contrasted the judge's attitude with that of His Father. God is the righteous Judge. While human beings often do things out of selfish motives, God is good and He rewards those who persist, persevere and plead their case before Him. Jesus is not saying that you need to put pressure on God, but that He wants to hear from you. Clearer yet, Jesus is saying, "How badly do you want what you are asking for?" Jesus is saying, "Do not give up!" We should pray all the time and not lose heart. Jesus assures us that God will administer justice "speedily" for His children. An unjust judge may drag his heels and take his time, but God won't. Keep pouring out your heart to God and be confident that the Lord will answer.

If you have a burning request, don't take no for an answer. Persist in your prayers and God will reward your faith. Will Jesus find faith in you? Can He trust you not to give up? Can He rely on you to be persistent and fervent in prayer? The apostle Paul reminds us, "Rejoice evermore. Pray without ceasing. In everything give thanks; for this is the will of God in Christ Jesus concerning you." [1Thes.5:16-18] Give thanks, ask and then wait. Just don't take no for an answer – Jesus invites you to keep praying.

Over To You

What have you been praying about for a long time?

_____

_____

_____

_____

What can you learn about prayer from the parable of the persistent widow?

_____

_____

_____

_____

What truths from God's Word will help you not to give up in prayer?

_____

_____

_____

_____

_____

_____

15

THE WOMAN WITH CONSTANT BLEEDING

EXTREME FAITH

"Daughter, your faith has healed you. Go in peace and be freed from your suffering."

Mark 5:34 (NIV)

Jesus had a crowd pressing about Him as he headed towards the home of Jairus, one of the Jewish leaders. In the midst of the hustle and bustle of the crowd, a woman who had been suffering constant bleeding – internal haemorrhaging – for twelve years saw her opportunity for healing in Jesus. The woman had spent all that she had seeking for a cure but now she found herself broke and, if anything, her condition had worsened. She reasoned that if she could just touch the hem of Jesus' clothes, she would be well, so she reached out and touched him. Immediately, her bleeding stopped and she felt in her body that she was freed from her suffering. Jesus recognised immediately that power had gone out from Him and asked who had touched His clothes. Then the woman, knowing what had happened to her, came and fell at His feet. Trembling with fear, she told Him the whole truth. Jesus lovingly said to her, "Daughter, your faith has healed you. Go in peace and be freed from your suffering." [Mk.5:34 (NIV)]

Have you been suffering from a longstanding issue? It could be a matter of your mental, spiritual or physical health, your finances, your home, your relationships or your career.

Sometimes, just like the woman, we can frantically try to sort out our own problems but are left feeling no better. Even the specialists may have failed you. Look out instead for Jesus. He isn't just passing by on His way to help someone else, He is available to help you too. If you could only get to Jesus, you know that ultimately every issue you ever have will be resolved. It is just a matter of getting to Him. Stretch, reach out and touch even the edge of His clothing. Recognise that your only hope for true healing is in Him. We won't necessarily receive immediate physical healing as this woman so wonderfully did, but Jesus will welcome you as He did the woman here and provide you the peace you need. And one day when He returns, we will be freed from all suffering.

Over To You

Are there any ways in which you identify with the woman in Mark 5?

_____

_____

_____

_____

_____

_____

What do we learn about Jesus in this story?

_____

_____

_____

_____

_____

_____

Spend some time reaching out to Jesus, telling him all your needs.

16

JAIRUS'S DAUGHTER

NOT DEAD, JUST SLEEPING

"Your daughter is dead," they said. "Why bother the teacher anymore?" Overhearing what they said, Jesus told him, "Don't be afraid; just believe."

Mark 5:35-36 (NIV)

In Mark 5 we read of a messenger who came from Jairus's house and told him that his daughter was dead. Why trouble Jesus any longer? Jesus overheard these words and said, "Don't be afraid; only believe." Then He continued on the way to Jairus's home. When He reached the house, Jesus came face to face with a group of mourners weeping and wailing. Jesus said to them, "What is all the noise about? Why are you crying? The child is not dead; she is only sleeping." Sorrow quickly turned to mockery, as the mourners laughed at Jesus scornfully. Jesus sent everyone except the parents out, took the child by the hand and said, "Little girl, get up." The little girl got up at the command of Jesus.

Jairus was confident that if Jesus came to his home and dealt with his personal emergency, then everything would turn out well. Have you been asking Jesus to come and lay His hands on your situation? It can seem that He has stopped to help someone else and has forgotten you. We may become frustrated and think Jesus doesn't realise the urgency of our situation. Doesn't He know that every second counts? Surely, He must know that your situation is a matter of life and death! Then the dreadful news arrives: death has reached the home before Jesus. So what now? Have you given up hope? Are you frustrated with Jesus' time management? Is He taking too long to deal with your situation when He seems to be taking care of everyone else?

Jesus will arrive at your situation at the right time. He will address whatever has been causing you suffering: that illness; that pain; the hope that lived within you, then died. When Jesus the resurrection and the life comes to your situation, He may well find death. Yet He requires you to exercise extreme faith. Believe that He can do what you asked. Do not be afraid when everyone else tells you that it is all over. Continue to 'bother' Jesus with your requests; He wants you to. Dismiss your friends and family members who are there to give you their reality checks. They may pronounce the situation dead and beyond revival; Jesus says that it is just sleeping, waiting for Him to come and wake it up. Whatever the situation you are facing, put yourself in God's presence. Humble yourself and beg Him to intervene.

Have confidence that God rewards the faith of everyone who comes to Him.

Over To You

Are you frustrated by God's seeming lack of urgency answering your prayers?

What do we learn about Jesus' timing from the story of Jarius's daughter?

How does this encourage us to trust Him?

17

MARY

WATER INTO WINE

His mother said to the servants, "Do whatever he tells you."
John 2:5 (NIV)

Have you ever been in a situation which required forethought, planning and resource management? You thought you had everything under control, but then, at the crucial moment, what you had was not enough. A sick feeling washes over you. Now what?

This was the situation in John 2. Unknown to most of the guests, the wine had just run out at the wedding. What would you have done in that situation? The young couple's relative goes and desperately mentions it to someone. Someone else might have come up with a plan to get to the nearest wholesale store, buy cheap drink and somehow tried to get it into the kitchen without the guests noticing. That presumes, of course, that they had the money to buy so much. What happens when the wine, the money, the time and just about everything else runs out? At a wedding with no wine, Jesus' mother did the only thing that she could do: she told Jesus. Jesus' response was a bit disappointing: "What does that have to do with Me? My time has not yet come." [Jn.2:4] Mary, however, said to the waiting staff, "Whatever He says to you, do it."

Do you have an urgent and embarrassing problem? Jesus' time may not have come the instant you want it to; however, when you need it, His timing will be just right. Having told Jesus your situation, whatever He tells you to do, just do it. Jesus said to the waiting staff that they should fill the empty jars nearby with water. Then He said that they should take some out and give it to the banqueting manager. On tasting the water which had turned into wine, the banqueting manager took the bridegroom aside and said, "People usually bring out the connoisseur and vintage products when the function first starts. Then later on, when the guests have had too much to drink and don't even notice or care what they are drinking, you bring out the cheap stuff. You, however, have saved the best wine until now!"

Are you running on empty? Do you need God to fill you up? Obey all Jesus tells us to do in His Word. Fill up your ordinary containers with your ordinary efforts. God will then exert His extraordinary power on what you have to offer. When it comes to the test, the guests invited or uninvited, the judges, critics and connoisseurs will all be forced to admit that what you have to offer exceeds their expectations. You will have saved the best wine for last.

Over To You

What would have been your response to the problem in John 2? What can we learn from Mary?

Are you running on empty? Do you need God to fill you up?

Are you ready to do whatever God says in His Word?

18

THE WOMAN AT THE WELL

DESPERATELY SEEKING

Jesus said to her, "Woman, believe Me, the hour is coming when you will neither on this mountain, nor in Jerusalem, worship the Father ... God is Spirit, and those who worship Him must worship in spirit and truth."

John 4:21,23 (NKJV)

No one in her community could quite make up their minds about who she was. The local women had a huge problem with her, as she had a reputation for enjoying male company a bit too much and her latest companion was a husband, just not hers. Some of the men in her community had no problem with this woman for precisely the same reason as the women did – she enjoyed male company very much. Thus, she found herself having to avoid the accusing eyes of the women of Sychar. In the heat of the day, she came to a well to draw water and found a man from out of town sitting there. It was Jesus and he asked her for a drink of water. The woman replied that as Jesus was obviously a Jew and she was quite clearly a Samaritan, surely He had no business asking *her* for a drink. Jesus responded that if she knew Who was asking and that He was Himself the gift of God, the roles would be reversed and she would be asking for living water. The woman observed that the man had no bucket or other utensil to collect water and said as much. Sceptical of His claims to have living water, she asked, "Where can you get this living water?" Jesus then told her about the living water He offered which would ensure that the one who drank would never be thirsty again. As someone who knew about insatiable appetites, she requested some of the water so that she need not return to the well for repeated visits.

Do you have a history of failed relationships? Do other women clutch their husbands and brandish their wedding rings when they see you? Is there some other embarrassing secret that makes people stop talking when you are close by? Do you have to avoid certain people because of a shared negative history? Do you long for someone to satisfy insatiable internal longings? Men from previous relationships could not do it, nor will the present one. Jesus pointed this out to the Samaritan woman. Perhaps He is pointing this out to you right now too. To all those who feel thirsty, weary, tired of the looks and the shame, Jesus offers water which will satisfy. You may not have a container, but if you desire God's living water, He will ensure that you are filled within with His Spirit. God is actively looking for someone who will worship in spirit and truth. You are just the sort of person He is seeking.

Over To You

Is there a void in your life?

_____

_____

_____

Where have you been looking for satisfaction?

_____

_____

_____

Are there things which have prevented you from worshipping God in spirit and truth?

_____

_____

_____

_____

_____

19

A WISE WOMAN

BRING MATTERS TO A HEAD

*A wise woman called from the city, "Listen! Listen! Tell Joab,
'Come here, I want to speak to you.' ... 'I am one of those who
are peaceable and faithful in Israel.'"*

2Sam.20:16,19 (ESV)

Sheba, a man from the tribe of Benjamin, happened to be at the gathering in Jerusalem. He sounded the trumpet and shouted, "We have no share in David ... Every man to his tent, Israel." [2Sam.20:1 (NIV)] So all the men of Israel deserted David to follow Sheba. Sheba passed through all the tribes of Israel gathering followers and ended up in a place called Abel Beth Maakah. The commander of David's army, Joab, came with his troops and besieged Sheba in Abel Beth Maakah. A woman from the city said to Joab, "We are the peaceful and faithful in Israel. You are trying to destroy a city that is a mother in Israel. Why do you want to swallow up the LORD's inheritance?" [2Sam.20:19 (NIV)] Joab replied that this was not his intention and that he merely wanted to capture Sheba. If the people of Abel handed over this one man, then Joab and his troops would withdraw. The woman said to Joab, "His head will be thrown to you from the wall." [2Sam.20:21] Then the woman went to all the people with her wise advice, and they cut off Sheba's head and threw it to Joab. Joab returned to the king in Jerusalem.

Despite the rejoicing at David's return to Jerusalem, there were still people who were not glad to see him back. Sheba had been vocal in his opposition and gained a following. He had not reckoned with Joab's military response to his treason. The wise woman within the city had been able to deal calmly with the situation and establish the root cause of the problem. She had assessed the likely long-term impact of the siege and found an appropriate response.

The wise woman has much to teach us about peaceful and faithful Christian living. We too can be besieged by the enemy. We too can entertain a traitor in our hearts: that bad habit, unhealthy relationship or temptation; that unkind or unforgiving spirit; or some other sin that could destroy us. Assess the situation. Remind yourself and the aggressor that you are one of God's peaceful and faithful children and will not accommodate traitors. In the name of Jesus, bring matters to a head. Then cast out the traitor immediately, so you can continue to live in peace and full assurance of faith in God.

Over To You

Do you have a reputation for being wise and thoughtful?

How can you keep a calm head when everyone is panicking?

What preparations can you make now that will help you deal decisively with trouble when the occasion demands it?

What traitors lurk in your heart which need to be thrown out?

20

HANNAH

SINGING HER SONG

"More are the children of the desolate than the children of the married woman," says the LORD.

Isaiah 54:1 (NKJV)

So it came to pass in the process of time that Hannah conceived and bore a son, and called his name Samuel, saying, "Because I have asked for him from the LORD."

1 Samuel 1:20 (NKJV)

On the day of her greatest sacrifice to the Lord, Hannah prayed from a heart which was overflowing with joy. Even though Hannah was giving up the precious gift of her son, she was overjoyed to do so because she was fulfilling her promise to God. Hannah thanked God for being her rock and strength. She acknowledged that through the power of God her whole life had turned around. She may have started out as the woman with the fertility issues, however now she was a proud mother. Hannah acknowledged the way that God reverses situations so that people who consider themselves rich are shown to be poor. People who feel that they are secure in powerful positions know what it is like to be humbled. At the same time, Hannah praised God for lifting her up and giving her a place of honour. She was *overflowing with praise*. Almost certainly, she was not rejoicing about leaving her son Samuel in the temple as she had promised to do, but she could and did rejoice in the Lord. In the most desperate situations, when you have nothing else to rejoice in, you must rejoice in the Lord.

We read in 1 Samuel 1 that Hannah had endured severe provoking from her 'rival' Peninnah during her years of childlessness before having Samuel. Have other people tormented or mocked you for being barren and unfruitful? "Sing, O barren, you who have not borne! Break forth into singing, and cry aloud, you who have not laboured with child! For more are the children of the desolate than the children of the married woman," says the LORD." [Is.54:1 (NKJV)] You have a song that only you can sing. Like Hannah, when God blesses you, smile defiantly at the Peninnahs of this world. Rejoice, because your Peninnahs may have brought you low but God has lifted you up. Without growing proud, walk boldly in God's favour because you are girded with His strength. Sing because you are not hungry anymore – your Heavenly Father has laid a table before you in the presence of your enemies. Sing, because by His grace, God has lifted you from the dust and He will set you among princes.

Over To You

Do you have a 'Penninah' in your life; a person bringing you down with their words?

_____

_____

_____

How does Hannah's example help you to know how to react?

_____

_____

_____

_____

_____

How can you celebrate in advance of God's victory for you?

_____

_____

_____

21

MANOAH'S WIFE

THIS WOMAN OF FAITH

...the Angel of the LORD appeared to the woman and said to her, "Indeed now, you are barren and have borne no children, but you shall conceive and bear a son."

Judges 13:3 (NKJV)

The Bible does not record her name; even her husband referred to her as "this woman". However, her faith shines out of her story. The Angel of God had visited and told Manoah's wife that her situation was about to change: she would have a child. Manoah wanted to get things right, so he prayed and asked God for further instructions as to how to raise the promised child. Specifically, he prayed for the man of God to visit again. God answered the prayer and the Angel of the Lord appeared and reiterated the previous instructions. Manoah was overjoyed at what he had heard and offered the stranger a meal. The Angel of the Lord declined the offer but told Manoah to sacrifice to the Lord.

Manoah offered a sacrifice of a young goat and a grain offering to God. The angel appeared to be engulfed by the flames, before disappearing from view, as Manoah and his wife looked on in awe. Finally, it dawned on them: they had been in the presence of a holy angel.

Manoah was horror-struck. "We are going to die because we have seen God!" he said.

However, his wife was not unduly concerned. "Why would the Lord appear to us, tell us such wonderful news and then accept our offerings if He were planning to kill us?"

Manoah had an encounter with God and was afraid that he was about to die. Manoah's wife came to a different conclusion. When you have an encounter with God, are you afraid or do you thank God that

He has revealed Himself to you? Manoah's wife was the voice of hope and reason. She urged her husband to look back and recount the blessings of God in the past. "Didn't God receive our burnt offering? Didn't He appear to us and tell us of this wonderful thing? Besides, hasn't He promised us so much for the future?"

As you reflect on the awesome revelation of God to you, remember that God has accepted your offering and that He has blessed you in the past. Moreover, He has performed miracles in your life and promised to bring forth deliverance in Him, from within your spiritual barrenness and brokenness. Hasn't He undeniably answered your prayers? God will accomplish, through you, this wonderful thing He has entrusted to you.

Over To You

Are you the voice of hope amidst doubt and unbelief?

_____

_____

_____

Will you trust God to deliver you from spiritual brokenness?

_____

_____

_____

Write down the wonderful things that you recognise that God has entrusted to you.

_____

_____

_____

_____

_____

_____

_____

22

ELIZABETH

WHEN GOD LOOKS AT YOU

Now after those days his wife Elizabeth conceived; and she hid
herself five months, saying, "Thus the Lord has dealt with me,
in the days when He looked on me, to take away my reproach
among people."

Luke 1:24-25 (NKJV)

Zechariah completed his days of service in the temple and then went home. Later his wife Elizabeth conceived; and *she hid herself away for five months*, saying, "Thus the Lord has dealt with me, *in the days when He looked on me*, to take away my reproach among people." [Lk.1:24-25 (NKJV), emphasis added] Elizabeth, the woman who everyone considered was past her best because she was no longer of childbearing age, became pregnant. Although this was a season of joy for her, she hid herself away from public view when she discovered her pregnancy. She kept herself hidden from the unkind looks and comments, until there was no way she could hide anymore. However, she did not need to worry about who was looking at her because God had already looked at her – with favour.

You may worry that people look down on you and consider you past your best and therefore redundant for their purposes. You may have that unsettling feeling that those around you look at you and talk about you behind your back. Are some even bold enough to talk about you in your hearing? The Lord is going to take away your reproach among people. For a while, it may be a secret thing between you and God. You may even consider it embarrassing to show the Lord's blessing in your life. What, at your age? In your time of life? However, there is no hiding the Lord's blessings indefinitely; all will be revealed in due time and there will be no way for your detractors to deny it. People may think that it is unfair. In your heart you will know, this is how God deals with people who are loyal to Him.

God just looks at His children, seeing their shame, their anxiety, whatever may be holding them back – and He restores them. Even though you may feel that you've been overlooked in the past, think again.

"For the eyes of the Lord search back and forth across the whole earth, looking for people whose hearts are perfect toward Him, so that He can show His great power in helping them." [2Chr.16:9, TLB] Stay devoted to God; His eyes are searching the earth and will bring you restoration in His perfect timing.

Over To You

Are you worried that life has passed you by?

_____

_____

How is it a comfort to know that God sees us and will restore us?

_____

_____

_____

_____

Write down those things that you are struggling with and then pray over them.

_____

_____

_____

_____

_____

_____

_____

23

MARY (1)

DARE TO BELIEVE

"For with God nothing will be impossible." Then Mary said, "Behold the maidservant of the Lord! Let it be to me according to your word."

Luke 1:37-38 (NKJV)

Six months after the angel Gabriel had spoken to Zachariah, he was sent by God to speak to a virgin called Mary, who was engaged to a man called Joseph.

Gabriel said to Mary, "Rejoice, you are highly favoured; the Lord is with you. You are a blessed woman!" Mary was confused about what Gabriel meant when he greeted her like this. The angel then said to her, "Do not be afraid, Mary, for you have found favour with God. You will conceive and give birth to a Son, and you will give Him the name Jesus. He will be great, and will be called the Son of the Highest."

Mary asked the angel, "How can that happen, as I am not married?"

Gabriel answered, "The Holy Spirit will come upon you, and the power of the Highest will overshadow you. ... Elizabeth your relative has conceived a son in her old age; and this is now the sixth month for her who was called barren. For with God nothing will be impossible." [Lk.1:35-37]

Mary replied, "I am your servant, Lord! Let it be to me according to your word." [Lk.1:38]

Six months had passed since the seemingly impossible had begun; Elizabeth, the barren woman, was now pregnant. Zachariah had displayed unbelief. Elizabeth had hidden herself away from the unkind speculation of the local people. Now Gabriel was speaking to Mary, and once again he was bringing incredible and unbelievable news. However, there was a subtle difference in Mary's response to the announcement she received. Zechariah had given Gabriel reasons as to why what God had promised could *not* happen. Mary wanted to know how it *would* happen. Mary's initial confusion over how she could be the one God had called – blessed and highly favoured – quickly gave way to acceptance that she was a vessel to be used by God.

Are you struggling with who you are called to be in Christ? In Christ, you too are blessed and highly favoured. Ask God to open your eyes to see the daily evidence that the Lord is with you. As His child, you are a blessed woman! God wants to fulfil his purposes through you too. Don't worry about the logistics. Dare to believe that you are who God says you are. With God, nothing is impossible.

Over To You

What makes you question God's means and methods?

_____

_____

_____

Are you struggling to find your God-given identity and purpose in life?

_____

_____

_____

Has God given you an 'impossible' vision for your life? Do you trust God to do the impossible in your life?

_____

_____

_____

_____

_____

24

MARY (2)

"BEHOLD YOUR MOTHER!"

When Jesus therefore saw His mother, and the disciple whom He loved standing by, He said to His mother, "Woman, behold your son!"

John 19:26 (NKJV)

There were four women standing near the cross: Jesus' mother, His mother's sister, Mary the wife of Cleopas and Mary Magdalene. When Jesus saw His mother and John, the disciple He loved, standing nearby, He said to His mother, "Woman, behold your son!" Then He said to the disciple, "Behold your mother!" And from that moment, John took Mary into his own home.

As believers, we are all at the foot of the cross. How are you feeling?

Are you like Mary, Jesus' mother, crushed, broken-hearted and in despair as you consider what life has done to your child or children?

Are you like Salome, Mary's sister, who had come to Jesus on behalf of her two sons, seeking places at His right hand for them [Matt.20:20-22]? Are you a woman ambitious for her children? Do you go to God on their behalf? Do you seek for them to have every advantage that perhaps you did not have?

Are you like Mary Magdalene, a carer, loving Jesus with all your heart, used and abused by men, not having any children of your own?

Are you like Mary the wife of Cleopas, behind the scenes, not really known but there with Jesus to the end?

There was one man at the cross, John the beloved disciple. He was there afraid, bewildered at the speed of what had taken place, but determined that no matter what happened, he would not lose sight of Jesus.

Five people, all at the cross, looking expectantly to Him. Then look at Jesus; in the hour when every other son would have thought about himself, Jesus thought about His mother. Jesus gave a powerful message to John: "Even when you are in crisis – reach out to and take care of those who nurtured you."

We may wonder why Jesus says what He does to John; after all, Mary had other children [Lk.8:19-21]. However, when Jesus asks you to care for a vulnerable person, He asks because He knows your strengths; He knows you can do it. Jesus was telling John that our relationships in Christ are more important than relationships of blood. As you look to Jesus today, look at the women around you and, as Jesus said, "Behold your mother."

Over To You

Of the people standing at the foot of the cross, whom do you identify with?

_____

_____

Are there ways you can care for the vulnerable women around you, especially other Christians?

_____

_____

_____

_____

_____

Are there ways you can better care for your own mother?

_____

_____

_____

_____

_____

25

JEHOSHEBA

A LITTLE-KNOWN WOMAN

But Jehosheba, the daughter of King Jehoram and sister of Ahaziah, took Joash son of Ahaziah and stole him away from among the royal princes.

2 Kings 11:2 (NIV)

Joash was sleeping in his nursery when the mayhem started. While the baby slept, his father King Ahaziah of Judah was killed and Athaliah, the queen mother, began to destroy the rest of the royal family. But Ahaziah's sister Jehosheba, the baby's aunt, took King Ahaziah's infant son Joash and stole him away from among the rest of the king's children, who were about to be killed. She put Joash and his nurse in a bedroom, and they hid him from the queen mother, so the child was not murdered. Joash remained hidden in the temple for six years while Athaliah ruled over the land.

Years earlier, King Jehoshaphat of Judah had made a political alliance with King Ahab of Israel by having his daughter marry Ahab's son. Now, with King Ahaziah dead, Athaliah was trying to save something for Ahab's family and for herself by attempting to eliminate the house of David in Judah. The line of David would have been wiped out, if it were not for the actions of one woman: Jehosheba. Amidst the bloodshed and the mayhem, Jehosheba rushed in to save the boy.

Most people will never have heard of Jehosheba. But through her brave and selfless actions, this relatively unknown woman allowed herself to be an instrument in God's hands to preserve the line of David, through which the promised Messiah would eventually come. Jehosheba probably did not realise how significant her act of service was to the kingdom of God.

Evil people will always have their schemes and plans, and for a while, they may even appear to succeed. However, God is always working out His plan. God always has His 'but' in a Jehosheba. As a believer, you are living and working in an environment which is hostile to the purposes of God. You may be unnoticed and unknown in the eyes of the world. However, like Jehosheba, you are God's servant in the right place at the right time. Ask God to give you the courage and concern of Jehosheba to reach out today in prayer and actions to help someone in need. Step out boldly and courageously; let God use you to snatch people from the deadly intentions of the enemy. You may not recognise the importance of your actions now, but God can use you to fulfil His promises to His people.

Over To You

In what ways is the environment you are living and working in hostile to the purposes of God?

_____

_____

_____

_____

_____

Are you willing to take the risk of doing the right thing to fulfil God's purposes?

_____

_____

_____

How does the story of Jehosheba encourage us that an ordinary believer, like you, can be a powerful instrument in God's hands?

_____

_____

_____

_____

26

HULDAH

MAKE YOUR MARK

Hilkiah and those the king had appointed went to Huldah the prophetess.

2 Chronicles 34:22 (NKJV)

Huldah was the wife of Shallum the keeper of the temple wardrobe. She lived in Jerusalem. King Josiah sent a delegation of men to meet with Huldah and ask her about the book they had found in the temple. She replied, "Tell the man who sent you that this is the message from God for him: God is going to destroy this place and there is no stopping what He intends to do. However, you must make sure that you deliver the following message to the king of Judah. God has taken note of the fact that you displayed genuine humility and repentance when you heard what He plans to do about this city. He acknowledges that you cried and desperately wanted to know what you could do to make amends. *God has heard your prayer.*" The delegation took Huldah's message back to the king.

Josiah has sent these men to enquire of the Lord. They did not go to the temple to ask the priest to explain God's Word. Nor did they go to visit Shallum, whose role was to look after the robes worn in the temple. Instead, they went to Shallum's wife, Huldah. As the wardrobe master's wife, it's likely that Huldah's main job was as a seamstress, assisting her husband in maintaining the robes. Huldah is not mentioned anywhere else in the story, yet somehow, when the people needed to hear a word from the Lord, they knew exactly where to go. The significant thing about Huldah was that the Lord was with her; He spoke to and through her, and everyone knew this, including Huldah herself.

We have God's precious Word, the Bible, in our possession. Let us be women of this Word so that when others need to hear from the Lord, we can tell them what He has said. Huldah gave her message, and retired from the scene, but she left her mark on her generation. She had fulfilled her mission. God gave Huldah a word for Josiah at a time when he needed to know that God hears His people when they are in despair. You may be just an ordinary person, just getting on with your normal routine, but you can speak life and hope as God directs you – be faithful in what God calls you to do.

Over To You

Do people know you as someone who listens to God through His Word?

_____

_____

_____

Are you willing to make yourself available for God to use you?

_____

_____

_____

Spend some time praying God would speak regularly to you in the Bible, and that you'd have wisdom in sharing His message with others.

27

TABITHA

AN UNDERVALUED 'DOER'

In Joppa there was a disciple named Tabitha (in Greek her name is Dorcas). Her life overflowed with good works and compassionate acts on behalf of those in need.

Acts 9:36 (CEB)

Who was Tabitha, this woman identified as a disciple and described as a generous supporter of the poor? By all accounts, Tabitha was a woman known for her good deeds, and when she died, the local community considered it to be a tragedy. Thus, they sent for Peter, who was in nearby Lydda, and persuaded him to come to Joppa. When Peter arrived at Tabitha's house, he found the widows weeping and showing tunics and other clothing that she had made while she was with them. Peter asked everyone to leave and prayed before telling Tabitha to rise up. This she did and she was restored to life and to her community.

It is sad but typical that Tabitha's life only came into focus when it had ended. One wonders whether the people crying when Peter arrived at the dead woman's home had ever taken the time to show appreciation for her generosity while she was alive to hear it. It appears that it was only when Tabitha died that the people who lived in her community recognised how valuable she was to them.

In today's world, with fashion designers providing cheap, ready to wear clothes, it is easy to overlook the effort and dedication which Tabitha showed. Hers was not the world of ready-cut patterns and sewing machines; Tabitha would have had to buy or weave the cloth, and spend time cutting fabrics and stitching by hand. But Tabitha's gift to her community was much more than sewing and distributing clothes. Tabitha gave something precious, something that so many people need:

her time. These were acts of love and service, examples of everyday good deeds, which were taken for granted until they were gone. Tabitha stands as a lesson to others in this busy, complicated world; she took the time to notice and to care. She stands as a call to us to notice the poor women who are desperately in need of help, living in our communities. She stands as an example of the impact one person's life can have when they choose to make a difference. What will your eulogy be?

Over To You

Who are the Tabithas in your life?

How can you appreciate other people and tell them so while they can still hear you?

Do you care for others? What is your legacy?

28

RHODA

KEEP ON INSISTING

When she recognized Peter's voice, she was so overjoyed she ran back without opening it and exclaimed, "Peter is at the door!"

Acts 12:14 (NIV)

King Herod seized the apostle Peter and put him in prison with a view to placing him on trial after the Passover. Meanwhile, the church was praying for Peter.

An angel entered the prison, released Peter's chains and walked him to freedom in the street. Peter then made his way to the house of Mary, the mother of John. When Peter knocked at the door, a servant girl named Rhoda answered. Recognising Peter's voice, in her joy she did not open the gate but ran in and reported that he was standing outside. They said to her, "You are out of your mind!" She kept insisting that Peter was there, but they kept saying, "It must be his angel."

Have you lived your life always 'knowing your place'? That was certainly Rhoda's experience. Her job was to serve in the house, not to make statements about it. Her job was to open the door – something that she neglected to do because of her excitement at hearing Peter's voice! Her job was to stay in the background, working behind the scenes, but somehow Rhoda found herself at the prayer meeting praying for Peter's release from prison. There were many fervent prayers offered for Peter's deliverance; everyone knew how cruel Herod could be. People prayed for a miracle, but when it happened they could not believe it.

How many times have people told you that you were out of your mind because what you were saying made no sense to them? How many times have you allowed yourself to be silenced because what you have been saying should not come from someone of your gender, culture or ethnic background, social position, financial status or some other standard? Rhoda would have none of it. The people who supposedly knew better than she did could say what they liked about her, she kept on insisting.

Have you experienced God's deliverance? Keep on insisting.

Do other people think you're crazy? Keep on insisting.

David could empathise with Rhoda. He said, "Show me a sign for good, that those who hate me may see it and be ashamed." [Ps.86:17 (NKJV)] Do you have proof of the goodness of God? Are other people sceptical? Whatever you do, keep on insisting.

Over To You

Are there ways you identify with Rhoda?

_____

_____

_____

_____

How can you continue to work behind the scenes but still let your voice be heard?

_____

_____

_____

_____

_____

How can you take courage from Rhoda's insistence in telling people what God has done?

_____

_____

_____

_____

REFLECTIONS

Now that you've reached the end of this devotional, what comes next? Take some time to reflect on the experiences of these women and how they can be applied to your life.

Spend time reading Proverbs 31 and 1 Samuel 2:1-10 to encourage yourself in the Lord. You can write your thoughts in the space below, recording all God is saying to you through them.

Remember to pray over your plans and delight yourself in the Lord so that He will grant you the desires of your heart (see Psalm 37:4). It is God's desire for you to be fruitful in your life.

Notes

RELATED BOOKS FROM THE PUBLISHER

Come Away With Me
Ruth Gregg

ISBN 978-1-78815-612-7

This 90-day devotional is an excellent resource to help us effectively engage with the Bible every day.

Ruth Gregg, Director of Impact Unlimited Bible College, draws our attention each day to a scripture, then clearly explains its meaning by relating it to our experiences in today's culture. Sometimes fun, always insightful, these short daily notes lead to a powerful application each day, helping us to grow into greater maturity in our relationship with the Lord.

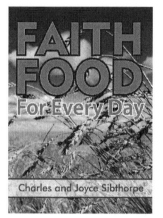

Faith Food for Every Day
Charles and Joyce Sibthorpe

ISBN 978-1-907509-63-6

Each day you will find a message that will encourage your faith, help with the challenge of the day ahead, and stir you to develop your personal relationship with God.

These messages appeared first in *Word for the Week*, sent by email around the world and published by *www.charlesandjoyce.com*.

Available from your local Christian bookshop
or from the publisher:

www.onwardsandupwards.org/**shop**